EUROPEAN COUNTRIES TODAY
SWEDEN

EUROPEAN COUNTRIES TODAY
TITLES IN THE SERIES

Austria	**Italy**
Belgium	**Netherlands**
Czech Republic	**Poland**
Denmark	**Portugal**
France	**Spain**
Germany	**Sweden**
Greece	**United Kingdom**
Ireland	**European Union Facts & Figures**

EUROPEAN COUNTRIES TODAY
SWEDEN

Dominic J. Ainsley

MASON CREST

Mason Crest
450 Parkway Drive, Suite D
Broomall, Pennsylvania PA 19008
(866) MCP-BOOK (toll free)

Copyright © 2019 by Mason Crest, an imprint of National Highlights, Inc. All rights reserved. No part of this publication may be reproduced or transmitted in any form or by any means, electronic or mechanical, including photocopying, recording, taping, or any information storage and retrieval system, without permission in writing from the publisher.
First printing
9 8 7 6 5 4 3 2 1

ISBN: 978-1-4222-3992-6
Series ISBN: 978-1-4222-3977-3
ebook ISBN: 978-1-4222-7807-9

Library of Congress Cataloging-in-Publication Data

Names: Ainsley, Dominic J., author.
Title: Sweden / Dominic J. Ainsley.
Description: Broomall, Pennsylvania : Mason Crest, 2019. | Series: European countries today | Includes index.
Identifiers: LCCN 2018007585 (print) | LCCN 2018016310 (ebook) | ISBN 9781422278079 (eBook) | ISBN 9781422239926 (hardback)
Subjects: LCSH: Sweden--Juvenile literature.
Classification: LCC DL609 (ebook) | LCC DL609 .A54 2019 (print) | DDC 948.5--dc23
LC record available at https://lccn.loc.gov/2018007585

Printed in the United States of America

Cover images
Main: *A view of the Stockholm archipelago.*
Left: *Swedish meatballs.*
Center: *Stockholm.*
Right: *Swedish folk dancers.*

QR CODES AND LINKS TO THIRD-PARTY CONTENT

You may gain access to certain third-party content ("Third- Party Sites") by scanning and using the QR Codes that appear in this publication (the "QR Codes"). We do not operate or control in any respect any information, products, or services on such Third-Party Sites linked to by us via the QR Codes included in this publication, and we assume no responsibility for any materials you may access using the QR Codes. Your use of the QR Codes may be subject to terms, limitations, or restrictions set forth in the applicable terms of use or otherwise established by the owners of the Third-Party Sites. Our linking to such Third-Party Sites via the QR Codes does not imply an endorsement or sponsorship of such Third-Party Sites or the information, products, or services offered on or through the Third-Party Sites, nor does it imply an endorsement or sponsorship of this publication by the owners of such Third-Party Sites.

CONTENTS

Sweden at a Glance	6
Chapter 1: **Sweden's Geography & Landscape**	11
Chapter 2: **The Government & History of Sweden**	25
Chapter 3: **The Swedish Economy**	45
Chapter 4: **Citizens of Sweden: People, Customs & Culture**	61
Chapter 5: **The Famous Cities of Sweden**	75
Chapter 6: **A Bright Future for Sweden**	85
Chronology	90
Further Reading & Internet Resources	91
Index	92
Picture Credits & Author	96

KEY ICONS TO LOOK FOR:

Words to Understand: These words with their easy-to-understand definitions will increase the reader's understanding of the text while building vocabulary skills.

Sidebars: This boxed material within the main text allows readers to build knowledge, gain insights, explore possibilities, and broaden their perspectives by weaving together additional information to provide realistic and holistic perspectives.

Educational Videos: Readers can view videos by scanning our QR codes, providing them with additional content to supplement the text. Examples include news coverage, moments in history, speeches, iconic sports moments, and much more!

Text-Dependent Questions: These questions send the reader back to the text for more careful attention to the evidence presented there.

Research Projects: Readers are pointed toward areas of further inquiry connected to each chapter. Suggestions are provided for projects that encourage deeper research and analysis.

SWEDEN AT A GLANCE

MAP OF EUROPE

The Geography of Sweden

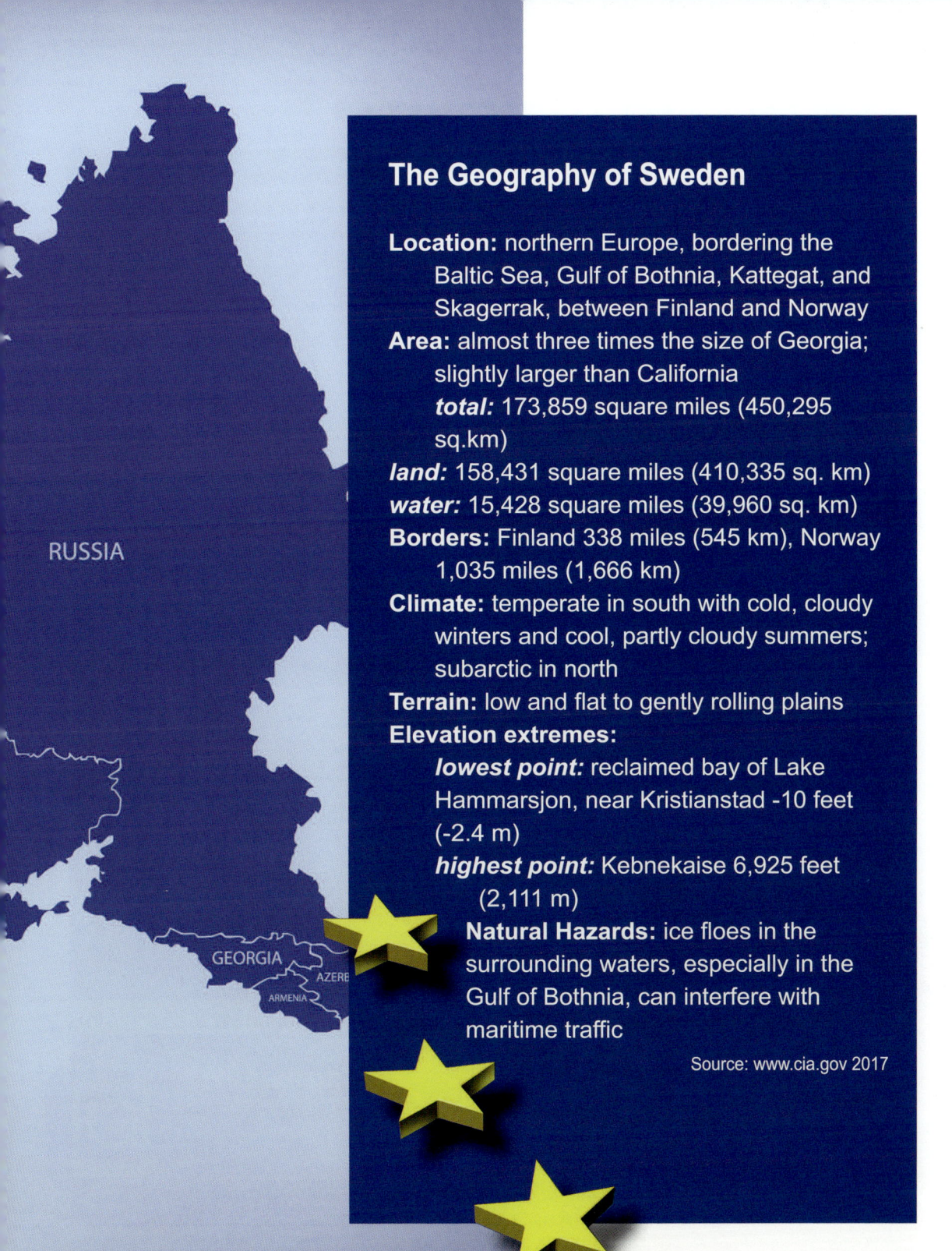

Location: northern Europe, bordering the Baltic Sea, Gulf of Bothnia, Kattegat, and Skagerrak, between Finland and Norway

Area: almost three times the size of Georgia; slightly larger than California
total: 173,859 square miles (450,295 sq.km)
land: 158,431 square miles (410,335 sq. km)
water: 15,428 square miles (39,960 sq. km)

Borders: Finland 338 miles (545 km), Norway 1,035 miles (1,666 km)

Climate: temperate in south with cold, cloudy winters and cool, partly cloudy summers; subarctic in north

Terrain: low and flat to gently rolling plains

Elevation extremes:
lowest point: reclaimed bay of Lake Hammarsjon, near Kristianstad -10 feet (-2.4 m)
highest point: Kebnekaise 6,925 feet (2,111 m)

Natural Hazards: ice floes in the surrounding waters, especially in the Gulf of Bothnia, can interfere with maritime traffic

Source: www.cia.gov 2017

SWEDEN AT A GLANCE

Flag of Sweden

Lying on the eastern half of the Scandinavian Peninsula, Sweden is a country of forests, plains, and lakes, much of which was shaped during the ice age. Sweden is one of the oldest kingdoms in Europe. It joined the European Union in 1995. The colors of the flag were taken from an ancient state coat of arms dating from the fourteenth century, although there is evidence to suggest that it was used from 1449 onwards. The off-center cross, common to all Scandinavian countries, derives from the flag of Denmark.

ABOVE: *The picturesque and historic neighborhood of Gamla Stan (Old Town) in Stockholm. It is one of the most visited parts of Stockholm.*

EUROPEAN COUNTRIES TODAY: SWEDEN

The People of Sweden

Population: 9,960,487
Ethnic groups: Swedes with Finnish and Sami minorities; most common countries of origin among immigrants: Finland, Syria, Iraq, Poland, Iran
Age structure:
　　0–14 years: 17.43%
　　15–24 years: 11.31%
　　25–54 years: 39.42%
　　55–64 years: 11.58%
　　65 years and over: 20.26%
Population grown rate: 0.81%
Birth rate: 12.1 births/1,000 pop.
Death rate: 9.4 deaths/1,000 pop.
Migration rate: 5.3 migrant(s)/1,000 pop.
Infant mortality rate: 2.6 deaths/1,000 live births
Life expectancy at birth:
　　Total population: 82.1 years
　　Male: 80.2 years
　　Female: 84.2 years
Total fertility rate: 1.88 children born/woman
Religions: Church of Sweden (Lutheran) 63%, other (includes Roman Catholic, Orthodox, Baptist, Muslim, Jewish, and Buddhist) 17% (2016 est.)
Languages: Swedish (official); Finnish, Sami, Romani, Yiddish, and Meänkieli are official minority languages
Literacy rate: 99%

Words to Understand

glaciers: Large bodies of ice moving slowly down a slope or valley.

ice age: A period of widespread glaciation.

populous: Full of residents or inhabitants.

BELOW: A view of Stockholm's Gamla Stan (Old Town).

Chapter One
SWEDEN'S GEOGRAPHY & LANDSCAPE

Sweden occupies the eastern portion of northern Europe's Scandinavian Peninsula. Slightly larger than the state of California, and nearly the same shape, Sweden is the largest and most **populous** nation in Scandinavia. The Swedes call their country *Sverige*, which means "the land of the Sveas," after the ancient inhabitants of the region. Stockholm is the country's capital and biggest city.

One of the northernmost nations, Sweden extends nearly 1,000 miles (1,600 kilometers) from north to south, and one-seventh of its territory lies above the Arctic Circle. Thick **glaciers** of the last **ice age** shaped the land, rounding mountaintops, carving out deep valleys, and digging long fjords into the coastline. Almost 100,000 lakes created by this glacial activity dot the countryside and cover about one-twelfth of the nation's total area.

ABOVE: *The small island of Rönnskär is situated in the Gulf of Bothnia, north Sweden.*

SWEDEN'S GEOGRAPHY & LANDSCAPE

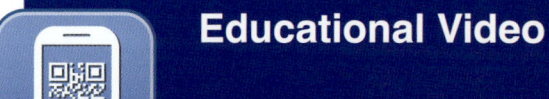

Educational Video

This video provides a brief insight into Sweden's geography. Scan the QR code with your phone to watch!

ABOVE: Unusual limestone formations on the island of Gotland.

EUROPEAN COUNTRIES TODAY: SWEDEN

ABOVE: *The Beach of Grenen is a sandbar at the junction between the strait of Skagerrak (part of the North Sea) and the Kattegat Sea.*

Sweden shares a hilly border with Norway to the west, and a narrow border with Finland to the northeast. The remainder of the nation borders the sea. The Gulf of Bothnia and the Baltic Sea lie to the east. Waterways separate Sweden from Denmark: the Skagerrak, Kattegat, and Öresund straits lie to the south and southwest. Two large islands in the Baltic Sea, Gotland and Öland, are also Swedish territories. Thousands of tiny, rock-covered islands are scattered along Sweden's Baltic coastline, protecting the mainland from the open sea.

Highlands, Marsh, and Woodlands

Sweden can be separated into three distinct regions: *Norrland*, or Northland, in the north; *Svealand*, or Land of the Swedes, in the center; and *Götaland*, or Land of the Goths, in the south.

SWEDEN'S GEOGRAPHY & LANDSCAPE

Kebnekaise

Situated in northern Sweden, Kebnekaise is the highest mountain in the country. The Kebnekaise massif lies within the Scandinavian mountain range and covers 200 square miles (500 square km). The mountain has two main peaks, the higher one is Mount Kebne at 6,926 feet (2,111 meters). Kebnekaise is very wild and uninhabited. It is known for its outstanding natural beauty. Kebnekaise is a popular tourist destination and is climbed by thousands each year. Some routes, however, require mountaineering equipment and other skills.

Norrland accounts for almost 70 percent of Sweden's land area but is home to only about 15 percent of the population. Far to the north, inside the Arctic Circle, is Samiland, a region inhabited by the Sami people. The land is largely treeless and barren, with extensive stretches of highlands that hold rich mineral deposits. Sweden's highest peak, Kebnekaise, rises to 6,926 feet (2,111 meters) in Samiland. The central area of Norrland is relatively flat and marked by marshlands, peat bogs, and dense stands of forest—mostly Scotch Pine and Norwegian Spruce. Long narrow lakes, rough stretches of river, and rocky glacial hills known as moraines interrupt the landscape. Further to the south, the land is more developed, and features agricultural and industrial regions with richer soils and Sweden's most important iron ore deposits.

EUROPEAN COUNTRIES TODAY: SWEDEN

Svealand is also heavily wooded, although more of this region has been cleared for farming and urban development, particularly around the cities of Stockholm and Uppsala. The land in central Svealand is generally low and flat with rich soil. Many of Sweden's largest lakes are located in Svealand.

In Götaland, south of the central lowlands, the land begins to rise and form the highlands of Småland. This area is similar to the moraine and peat bog region of Norrland, except that it has a warmer climate. At the southern edge of Sweden, the land drops again to form the low agricultural plain of the province of Skåne. This highly developed agricultural region is densely populated and is known as Sweden's breadbasket.

ABOVE: *Kiruna is situated in the north of Sweden in the province of Lapland. The town grew up around a large iron ore mine. Over the years, the mine (located close by) had undermined parts of the town. In 2014, the municipal council started to move parts of the town to a safer location. This work is ongoing.*

SWEDEN'S GEOGRAPHY & LANDSCAPE

ABOVE: *A rape seed crop in Skåne, which is the southernmost county in Sweden.*

Southeast of Stockholm in the Baltic Sea are Sweden's two largest islands, Öland and Gotland. Öland, covering 519 square miles (1,344 square kilometers), and Gotland, covering 1,210 square miles (3,140 square kilometers), are generally flat. The islands have a maritime climate and are home to a great variety of unusual plants. Sandy beaches can be found in many places, making the islands popular vacation destinations. Many smaller islands can also be found in the waters off the Swedish coast.

EUROPEAN COUNTRIES TODAY: SWEDEN

Rivers and Lakes

Sweden has about 100,000 lakes and many rapid, turbulent rivers. Most major rivers are in Norrland and flow in a southeasterly direction toward the Gulf of Bothnia and the Baltic Sea. The rivers, which are often connected to long, narrow lakes, are a valuable source of hydroelectric power. They are also used as an important means of transport for logs in Sweden's thriving lumber industry. Sweden's principal rivers are the Ångermanälven, Dalälven, Trysilelva, Umeälven, and Torneälven.

ABOVE: *Höga Kusten or High Coast Bridge crosses the mouth of the Ångermanälven River in the east of Sweden.*

SWEDEN'S GEOGRAPHY & LANDSCAPE

ABOVE: Lake Vänern is situated next to Läckö Castle, which is near the town of Lidköping, in Västra Götaland County.

In the south-central area of the country, known as the lake district, are two lakes: the Vänern, which covers 2,156 square miles (5,584 square kilometers), is Europe's third-largest lake; the Vättern, which covers 740 square miles (1,910 square kilometers), is Sweden's second-largest lake, after Vänern. The two lakes, together with several smaller lakes, rivers, and canals, form an important domestic water route called the Göta Canal. Originally built in the early nineteenth century, the Göta Canal extends for about 240 miles (about 386 kilometers) and provides a critical transportation link between the Baltic Sea, Stockholm, and other cities. Other important lakes in the district include Mälaren, Hjälmaren, and Siljan.

EUROPEAN COUNTRIES TODAY: SWEDEN

A Varied Climate

Although a significant portion of Sweden's land lies north of the Arctic Circle, the Swedish climate is much milder than that of most other countries located equally as far north. Sweden's relatively moderate climate results from the warming influence of winds blowing across the Gulf Stream, which sweep over Sweden from the North Atlantic Ocean. In winter, these warming influences are offset by cold air masses that come in from the north and east.

Northern Sweden's climate is much more severe than that of the south, primarily because elevations are higher and the mountains block the warming

ABOVE: *Ice floes in the Baltic Sea, near Sundsvall, in Västernorrland County.*

SWEDEN'S GEOGRAPHY & LANDSCAPE

marine winds. The average temperature in February, the coldest month, is in the below freezing range in Stockholm of 22 degrees to 30 degrees F (-5 degrees to -1 degrees C), in Göteborg of 25 degrees to 34 degrees F (-4 degrees to 1 degree C), and in Piteå, in the northern part of the country, of 6 degrees to 22 degrees F (-14 degrees to -6 degrees C). In July, the warmest month, the average temperature range is 56 degrees to 69 degrees F (13 degrees to 21 degrees C) in Göteborg, and 53 degrees to 69 degrees F (12 degrees to 21 degrees C in Piteå. North of the Arctic Circle, daylight is continuous for about two months in summer, while continuous darkness occurs for about two months in winter. Ice covers all lakes for more than a hundred days a year in the far north. The Gulf of Bothnia typically begins to freeze over near the shore in late November, and the ice usually lasts until the approach of the summer in June. Fog is common all along the Swedish coastline.

ABOVE: *Fjällbacka is a popular summer tourist destination. The town is situated in Västra Götaland County.*

EUROPEAN COUNTRIES TODAY: SWEDEN

Cormorant

The cormorant is a common species found in Sweden along seashores and in lakes and reservoirs, where its skill at catching fish often causes it to come into conflict with anglers. A generally long-necked, almost snake-like, bluish-black bird, but with attractive subtle marbling on its wings and a large yellow bill, the cormorant also has white cheeks and thigh patches when breeding. It swims well, rarely venturing far from land, and dives from the surface to hunt for fish, bringing big prey to the surface before swallowing it. After a fishing expedition the cormorant will often find a suitable wooden post, rock, or similar elevated site on which to perch. Cormorants breed in colonies, with nests often built on trees or cliffs.

Precipitation is relatively low across the country, except in the higher mountainous regions. Rainfall is heaviest in the mountains along the Norwegian border and in the southwest. Most rain falls in the late summer. During the winter months, heavy snows are common in central and northern Sweden.

Trees, Plants, and Wildlife

Arctic vegetation prevails in northern Sweden. The highest mountain areas are barren of vegetation. The next-highest regions are the moorlands, which are inhabited by various kinds of mosses, lichens, and a few species of hardy flowering plants. South of the moorlands is an area of birch and willow trees;

SWEDEN'S GEOGRAPHY & LANDSCAPE

although, because of the harsh conditions, these trees are often dwarfed and stunted. The next lower, and largest region, is covered with coniferous forest. This immense forest belt stretches across more than six hundred miles (950 kilometers) with a width that ranges from 100 miles to more than 150 miles (160 kilometers to more than 240 kilometers). In the south, deciduous trees, such as oak, beech, elm, and maple, can be found. On the islands of Gotland and Öland, the mild climate encourages the growth of walnut, acacia, and mulberry trees.

Roe deer and moose are common in Swedish forests. Reindeer are common in the north, where they are herded by the Sami. Bears, lynx, and wolves,

ABOVE: A herd of reindeer in northern Sweden.

EUROPEAN COUNTRIES TODAY: SWEDEN

although once plentiful, are now quite rare. Lemmings are plentiful in the northern moorlands. Various wild birds are abundant, with many rare species protected on nature preserves.

Fish thrive in the North and the Baltic seas and in Sweden's lakes and rivers. Principal marine varieties include mackerel, herring, and cod; freshwater varieties include pike, perch, whiting, and trout. Salmon are found in both fresh- and salt water. Shellfish, including lobsters and prawns, are found in coastal waters. Thousands of seals live in the waters around Sweden. In 1988, an outbreak of a deadly disease called phocine distemper virus (PDV) wiped out as much as 65 percent of the seal population in the North and Baltic seas. Thankfully, in recent years the seal population has largely bounced back. Sweden has adopted EU standards for environmental protection and operates several national parks and protected nature areas.

Text-Dependent Questions

1. What is the capital city of Sweden?

2. What is the highest mountain in Sweden?

3. How many lakes are there in Sweden?

Research Project

Imagine you are on vacation in Sweden. Write a journal describing your travels. What places do you think are important to visit and why?

Words to Understand

sovereign: Having independent authority and the right to govern itself.

tribe: A group of people that includes many families and relatives who have the same language, customs, and beliefs.

Viking: A member of a group of Scandinavian people who attacked the coasts of Europe in the eighth to tenth centuries CE.

BELOW: The Ale's Stones at Kåseberga, Österlen, is Sweden's best-preserved megalithic monument. It comprises fifty-nine standing stones laid in a shape of a ship. The monument is 1,400 years old.

Chapter Two
THE GOVERNMENT & HISTORY OF SWEDEN

Sweden is an ancient country that has existed as an independent and **sovereign** nation for hundreds of years. Signs of human habitation can be found in Sweden dating back to 9000 BCE. Sweden has a high concentration of ancient petroglyphs from that era that can be found all across the country. A petroglyph is an image carved by prehistoric peoples on natural rock surfaces. These images are thought to be the earliest form of nonwritten communication. The earliest images can be found in the northern province of Jämtland, depicting the hunt for wild animals such as elk, reindeer, bears, and seals.

Sweden in the Iron Age

In 98 CE, the Roman historian Tacitus described a **tribe** of people called the Suiones living on an island in sea. These Suiones had ships that were noteworthy because of their distinctive shape with a prow on both ends. Today, we recognize that shape as the classic **Viking** ship. The

ABOVE: *A petroglyph dating back about 4,000 years, near Nyköping in Södermanland County.*

25

THE GOVERNMENT & HISTORY OF SWEDEN

Educational Video

Top ten facts about Vikings.

The name Suiones corresponds to the peoples the Anglo-Saxons knew as Sweons whose country was called Sweoland. In the epic *Beowulf*, this tribe is also called Sweoeod.

By the sixth century, the Ostrogoth historian Jordanes also wrote about the Suiones. Several independent historical sources mention a number of Swedish kings who lived during this period. At that time, kings were warlords rather than kings as we understand that title today, and their lands were a number of petty kingdoms whose borders changed constantly as the kings battled and killed each other. The politics of these early kingdoms are retold in *Beowulf* and the Norse sagas.

The period between 793 and 1066 is known as the Viking Age. This corresponds to the latter half of the Iron Age. During this period, the Vikings, who

ABOVE: *The first page of the heroic epic poem* Beowulf, *written primarily in the West Saxon dialect of Old English.*

EUROPEAN COUNTRIES TODAY: SWEDEN

were warriors and traders from Sweden, Denmark, and Norway, raided and explored large parts of Europe, the Middle East, northern Africa, and even the coast of North America.

The longships used by the Vikings were the most technologically sophisticated of their day. Uniquely suited to both deep and shallow waters, these ships extended the reach of Norse raiders, traders, and settlers not only along coastlines but also along the major rivers of Europe. The Viking leader Rurik founded the first Russian state, with a capital at Novgorod. Other explorers from modern-day Sweden continued south on rivers to the Black Sea and went on to establish trade with Constantinople.

Swedish Vikings also played a role in western Europe later in the Viking period. During the conquest of England under the Danish king Svein Forkbeard, Swedes, along with Norwegians, were recruited as mercenaries to aid in the invasion. Monuments in Sweden attest to the skill of warriors who returned

ABOVE: *The royal mounds at Gamla Uppsala are around 1,400 years old. According to the Ynglinga saga, the kings Aun, Egil, and Adils were buried in Old Uppsala (Gamla Uppsala). One interpretation is that the kings are buried in the three great mounds at the site.*

THE GOVERNMENT & HISTORY OF SWEDEN

home rich in plunder from English campaigns. Later on, Swedes were recruited by the infamous Norwegian king Harald to help him regain control of Norway. These Swedish mercenaries subsequently helped Harald to invade England in 1066, where he and his army were destroyed, marking the end of the Viking Age.

Christianization and the Early Swedish Kings

At around the beginning of the ninth century, historical records note a king named Erik, whose kingdom seems to have reached as far as Norway. Later, another king named Björn is said to have been the son of Erik and to have reigned fifty years. Björn's successors were his sons Olof and Eric, also known as Eric the Victorious. Following Olof's death, his son Styrbjörn was refused his share of power by Eric. Eventually, Styrbjörn attacked Eric, and a battle took place between the two in which Styrbjörn was defeated and killed. Eric himself died ten years after this battle, apparently about 993. According to the story, be had obtained victory from the god Odin in return for a promise to give himself to the gods at the end of ten years.

ABOVE: A relief dating to c.1200 of Harald being baptized by Poppo the Monk.

ABOVE: King Magnus of Sweden.

EUROPEAN COUNTRIES TODAY: SWEDEN

Eric's son Olof succeeded him as king and instituted Christianity as the state religion. For the next 280 years, the land was ruled by a series of kings who gained and lost territory through long years of almost unending warfare. During this period, the newly Christian Swedes broke with the Roman Catholic Church and established the Church of Sweden. By 1275, the Swedish king, Magnus Ladulås found himself the leader of a heavily divided nation. Lesser rulers waged constant battles over small tracts of land, and the security of Swedish territory was threatened by enemies abroad who sought to take advantage of the country's instability.

ABOVE: Queen Margaret of Demark and Sweden. The photograph is of her tomb in Roskilde Cathedral, Denmark.

King Magnus introduced a feudal system similar to that already established elsewhere in Europe, and, as a result, the warring factions of Sweden were once more reunited. Magnus also promoted the formation of separate classes by extending the privileges of the clergy and instituting the landed nobility. Knights (lesser nobles and men of the upper-middle class) now formed a heavily armed cavalry as the core of the national army. The period of Magnus's reign marks the rise of a prominent merchant class, as the towns now began to acquire charters. By the beginning of the fourteenth century, codified laws appeared, and the king and his council began to perform legislative functions.

Unfortunately, after the king's death, some of the instability returned as different nobles fought for the throne. The Swedes were briefly united with Norway in 1319, but various petty power struggles continued as a succession of kings were supplanted by their nephews and cousins. Eventually, at the request of the Swedish nobility, the Swedes formed an alliance with Queen

THE GOVERNMENT & HISTORY OF SWEDEN

Margaret I of Denmark, becoming subjects of the Danish throne in what became known as the Kalmar Union.

The Kalmar Union

The Kalmar Union was formed by Queen Margaret I of Denmark in the Swedish town of Kalmar, then close to the Danish border. The Swedish king Albert, born in Germany, was disliked by the Swedish nobility, and their rebellion had received help from the Danes, who intended the union to serve as protection from the growing power of the Germans. As a result, Margaret united the three kingdoms of Denmark, Norway, and Sweden under a single monarch.

Eventually, the Swedes became unhappy with the Danes' frequent wars, which were a disturbance to Swedish commerce. Also, the centralization of government in Denmark caused resentment. The Swedish nobility wanted to retain a substantial degree of self-government. The union began to dissolve in 1430, and, ultimately, an armed rebellion led to the expulsion of Danish forces from Sweden. When the current king died childless in 1448, Sweden elected Charles VIII as their king, with the intent of reestablishing the union under a Swedish crown. Charles was elected king of Norway in the following year, but the counts of Holstein were more influential than the Swedes and the Norwegians together, and

ABOVE: *King Albert of Sweden.*

ABOVE: *King Christian II.*

EUROPEAN COUNTRIES TODAY: SWEDEN

they made the Danes appoint Christian I of Oldenburg as king. The ensuing struggle for power between Sweden and Denmark dominated the union for another seventy years.

Ultimately, the harsh policies of the Danes led to the end of their rule of Sweden. After the bloody retaking of Sweden by Christian II in 1520, and the subsequent massacre of Swedish patriots, known as the Stockholm Bloodbath, the Swedes started yet another revolt in 1521, which ousted the Danish forces once and for all. Independence was regained with the election of King Gustav Vasa on June 6, 1523, thereby restoring sovereignty for Sweden and finally dissolving the Kalmar Union.

The Rise of Swedish Power

Gustav fought for an independent Sweden, crushing attempts to restore the Kalmar Union and laying the foundations of modern Sweden. At the same time,

ABOVE: The Entry of King Gustav Vasa of Sweden into Stockholm, *1523 by Carl Larsson.*

THE GOVERNMENT & HISTORY OF SWEDEN

ABOVE: *Martin Luther (1483–1546). Portrait by Lucas Cranach the Elder.*

he broke with the Catholic Church. In 1517, Martin Luther, a German monk, led a revolt against the Roman Catholic Church. Lutheranism, the religious philosophy established by Luther, quickly gained a following across Europe. When the Roman Catholic Church supported the Danish king as the rightful ruler of Sweden, Gustav declared a split with Rome and appointed his own bishops to institute Lutheran reforms in the Church of Sweden. He also seized all church holdings, thus stripping Rome of its wealth and influence in Sweden.

During the seventeenth century, Sweden emerged victorious in wars against Denmark-Norway, Russia, and Poland. Sweden, with about one million inhabitants, was beginning to emerge as a major European power. Following the Peace of Westphalia in 1648, Sweden ruled the Russian province of Ingria (in which Saint Petersburg later would be founded), Estonia, Livonia, and even some major coastal towns and other areas of northern Germany. By 1658, Sweden had also acquired important provinces in Denmark and Norway.

The increasing wealth and power of the Swedes did not go unnoticed by their neighbors. Russia, Poland, and Denmark-Norway formed a military alliance in 1700 and attacked the Swedish Empire. Although the young Swedish king Charles XII won some important victories in the early years of the Great Northern War, his decision to attack Russia proved disastrous. With Swedish forces spread too thinly to adequately defend all fronts, the Swedes began to experience a series of defeats.

King Charles was killed during a battle in Norway in 1718. At the war's end, the allied powers, joined by Prussia and England, ended Sweden's brief period of glory by seizing her foreign holdings and introducing a fifty-year period of limited monarchy under parliamentary rule. In 1772, a bloodless coup d'état led by King Gustav III resulted in the return of absolute monarchy, a state of affairs that would last until limited monarchy returned following Sweden's involvement in the Napoleonic Wars of the nineteenth century.

Modernization of Sweden

The late nineteenth century was an important period of modernization and industrialization for Sweden. The nation's predominantly agricultural economy began to shift to a more industrialized economy.

ABOVE: *King Gustav III of Sweden.*

Unfortunately, wealth and prosperity did not increase at the same rate as the population. About one million Swedes immigrated to the United States between 1850 and 1890.

Many important developments occurred during this period of Swedish history, including the foundation of a modern free press, the abolition of trade monopolies in manufacturing to better promote free enterprise, the reform of national taxation and voting laws, the introduction of national military service, and the beginning of a multi-party political system. By the end of the century, three major political parties operated in Sweden: the Social Democrat Party, the Liberal Party, and the Conservative Party.

As the twentieth century dawned, the nation saw even greater changes. Industry continued to grow in importance to the national economy. Suffrage was expanded to include all men over the age of twenty-one, and sweeping

THE GOVERNMENT & HISTORY OF SWEDEN

ABOVE: *Swedish Prime Minister Per Albin Hansson declared Sweden neutral on September 1, 1939.*

labor reforms were made to improve working conditions in factories and to limit the long hours worked by children. Sweden was once again growing in prosperity and influence when World War I swept across Europe.

World War I began on June 28, 1914, when Gavrilo Princip, a Serbian nationalist, assassinated Archduke Ferdinand and his wife Sophie of Austria. Russia allied with Serbia. Germany sided with Austria and soon declared war on Russia. After France declared its support for Russia, Germany attacked France. German troops then invaded Belgium, a neutral country, as it stood between German forces and Paris. Great Britain eventually declared war on Germany. Soon, the United States and other nations around the world were at war. Because of Sweden's out-of-the-way location, as well as the high demand on both sides for Swedish steel, ball bearings, wood pulp, and matches, Sweden was able not only to remain neutral throughout the conflict but also to profit from it.

The wealth accumulated during the war helped to buffer the effects of the worldwide depression that struck in the 1930s. During this period, the Swedes instituted many welfare policies regarding financial assistance for the unemployed, the disabled, and the elderly, which are the foundations of the modern welfare state seen in Sweden today.

Another result of World War I was the recognition by Sweden that declaring neutrality during a time of war was not necessarily a guarantee of escaping the conflict. Having seen the invasion and occupation of other neutral territories during the war, Sweden began to invest in its military, determined to have the equipment and manpower to defend itself in the face of foreign invasion. This proved to be very insightful planning.

World War II and Sweden Today

As Sweden increased its social welfare structure and military capabilities, the hardships faced in other parts of Europe that were devastated by the Great Depression caused great unrest. In Germany, the Nazi Party grew powerful, attracting members by offering radical solutions to the country's economic problems and upholding patriotic values. The Nazis' leader, Adolph Hitler, had ambitious plans for Germany's future.

THE GOVERNMENT & HISTORY OF SWEDEN

ABOVE: *An abandoned World War II bunker in Vaermland.*

EUROPEAN COUNTRIES TODAY: SWEDEN

ABOVE: A Swedish soldier during World War II.

ABOVE: King Gustav III of Sweden.

Soon after being appointed chancellor of Germany in 1933, Adolf Hitler became a dictator. Hitler wanted to rebuild the German military power it had lost in World War I. In 1936, he formed an alliance with Italy and signed an anti-Communist agreement with Japan. These three powers became known as the Axis Powers. France, Great Britain, and the countries that were allied with them became known simply as the Allies.

Hitler's stated goal of reclaiming German lands lost in World War I was initially accepted by the Allies, and a policy known as appeasement was developed that granted a series of concessions to Hitler in hopes of preventing another war. This ultimately proved unsuccessful, and Hitler's armies swept across Europe as World War II began.

Sweden once again proclaimed its neutrality in the conflict. However, Swedish policy during World War II had some distinct differences from the policies pursued during World War I. This time, the Swedes engaged in a policy known as armed neutrality. This meant that the draft was in effect, and all able-bodied soldiers were called up to join the armed forces in case of foreign invasion. To pacify Nazi aggression, the Swedes allowed German troops to make use of a few railroads for transporting men and supplies, and Sweden continued to trade with both sides throughout the war.

THE GOVERNMENT & HISTORY OF SWEDEN

The Swedish policy of armed neutrality may have been the only thing that saved the country from foreign invasion and occupation. The Germans considered invading Sweden because they coveted the nation's factories, natural resources, and ports. The Allies considered invasion as a staging point for a further invasion of German-occupied Europe. In the end, both sides decided that the wiser course of action was to maintain trade and diplomatic relations and avoid armed conflict with the well-prepared Swedish forces. Sweden was able once again to avoid a conflict that devastated much of the wider world.

Following World War II, Sweden expanded its industrial sector to supply the rebuilding of Europe, leading to Sweden becoming one of the richest countries

Nordic Council

The Nordic Council is the official body for formal inter-parliamentary cooperation between the Nordic countries. It was formed in 1952 after World War II to promote collaboration between the five Nordic countries. Its first concrete result was the introduction in 1952 of a common labor market and free movement across borders without passports for the countries' citizens.

The Council consists of 87 representatives from Denmark, Finland, Iceland, Norway, and Sweden, as well as the autonomous areas of the Faroe Islands, Greenland, and the Åland Islands. The Council holds ordinary sessions each year in October/November and usually one extra session per year with a specific theme. Since 1991 Estonia, Latvia, and Lithuania participate with observer status, as well as the German state of Schleswig-Holstein since 2016.

EUROPEAN COUNTRIES TODAY: SWEDEN

ABOVE: *King Carl XVI Gustaf (left) and Queen Silvia of Sweden on a visit to Berlin in 2016.*

THE GOVERNMENT & HISTORY OF SWEDEN

ABOVE: Stockholm Palace is the official residence of the Swedish monarch. It is located in Gamla Stan (Old Town), Stockholm.

EUROPEAN COUNTRIES TODAY: SWEDEN

in the world by 1960. As a result of maintaining peace and neutrality for the entire twentieth century, Sweden has achieved an enviable standard of living. Governed under a social democratic system, the Swedes enjoy the many advantages of a high-tech economy and extensive social welfare system.

Because Swedes see their current prosperity as being directly linked to peace, the nation is still not a member of any military alliance. However, the country is anxious to maintain solid economic and political ties with its neighbors, which led to Sweden joining the European Union in 1995. This move had economic as well as political implications for the nation.

Sweden's current prime minister is Stefan Löfven, leader of the Social Democratic Party. Löfven grew up as foster child in a working-class family in Ådalen, Västernorrland, in northeastern Sweden. He has been in office since 2014.

Text-Dependent Questions

1. What is a petroglyph?

2. What does armed neutrality mean?

3. When did Sweden join the European Union?

Research Project

The policy of neutrality during the world wars helped Sweden to create dramatic economic growth. Write a report on Sweden's trade during wartime.

THE GOVERNMENT & HISTORY OF SWEDEN

The Formation of the European Union (EU)

The EU is a confederation of European nations that continues to grow. As of 2017, there are twenty-eight official members. Several other candidates are also waiting for approval. All countries that enter the EU agree to follow common laws about foreign security policies. They also agree to cooperate on legal matters that go on within the EU. The European Council meets to discuss all international matters and make decisions about them. Each country's own concerns and interests are important, though. And apart from legal and financial issues, the EU tries to uphold values such as peace, human dignity, freedom, and equality.

All member countries remain autonomous. This means that they generally keep their own laws and regulations. The idea for a union among European nations was first mentioned after World War II. The war had devastated much of Europe, both physically and financially. In 1950, the French foreign minister suggested that France and West Germany combine their coal and steel industries under one authority. Both countries would have control over the

ABOVE: *The entrance to the European Union Parliament Building in Brussels.*

EUROPEAN COUNTRIES TODAY: SWEDEN

Member Countries

Austria	Greece	Romania
Belgium	Hungary	Slovakia
Bulgaria	Ireland	Slovenia
Croatia	Italy	Spain
Cyprus	Latvia	Sweden
Czech Republic	Lithuania	United Kingdom
Denmark	Luxembourg	*(Brexit: For the time*
Estonia	Malta	*being, the United*
Finland	Netherlands	*Kingdom remains a full*
France	Poland	*member of the EU.)*
Germany	Portugal	

industries. This would help them become more financially stable. It would also make war between the countries much more difficult. The idea was interesting to other European countries as well. In 1951, France, West Germany, Belgium, Luxembourg, the Netherlands, and Italy signed the Treaty of Paris, creating the European Coal and Steel Community. These six countries would become the core of the EU.

In 1957, these same countries signed the Treaties of Rome, creating the European Economic Community. In 1965, the Merger Treaty formed the European Community. Finally, in 1992, the Maastricht Treaty was signed. This treaty defined the European Union. It gave a framework for expanding the EU's political role, particularly in the area of foreign and security policy. It would also replace national currencies with the euro. The next year, the treaty went into effect. At that time, the member countries included the original six plus another six who had joined during the 1970s and '80s.

In the following years, the EU would take more steps to form a single market for its members. This would make joining the union even more advantageous. In addition to enlargement, the EU is steadily becoming more integrated through its own policies for closer cooperation between member states.

Words to Understand

coniferous: Relating to, or belonging to, the plant phylum *Coniferophyta*.

cooperatives: Jointly owned enterprises engaging in the production or distribution of goods or the supplying of services, operated by its members for their mutual benefit.

hydroelectric: Pertaining to the generation and distribution of electricity derived from the energy of water.

BELOW: In summer, Sweden has the advantage of having long hours of daylight, which ensures a good harvest. This barley field, with a cottage in the background, is situated on Lake Vättern. By contrast, in midwinter in the far north of the country, there is around-the-clock darkness.

Chapter Three
THE SWEDISH ECONOMY

Sweden is a heavily industrialized country. Agriculture, once accounting for almost all of Sweden's economy, now employs about 2 percent of the labor force. Vast forests, rich iron deposits, and the wide availability of **hydroelectric** power are important natural resources; through the application of technology and efficient organization, they have enabled Sweden to become one of Europe's leading producing and exporting nations.

ABOVE: *A pile of birch lumber in a Swedish forest. Wood is used for furniture, construction, and pulped for paper products.*

THE SWEDISH ECONOMY

Forestry

Wood is Sweden's most important natural resource. The land is rich in timber, and many valuable **coniferous** softwoods are grown in Sweden, as well as a variety of less valuable hardwoods and several varieties of spruce and pine. The majority of Sweden's forests are privately owned by small farmers or form part of larger estates, while a smaller area belongs to the state, the church, and local **cooperatives**. The remainder are owned by major sawmilling and pulp corporations. These corporate forests, which are among the best managed in the country, lie mainly in the sparsely populated north.

ABOVE: Värmland County has many lakes and dense forests.

EUROPEAN COUNTRIES TODAY: SWEDEN

IKEA

Now based in the Netherlands, IKEA is a Swedish-founded multinational group that designs and sells ready-to-assemble furniture, kitchen appliances, and virtually every accessory you would ever need for a home. Ikea shops can be found in a great number of countries, and, in fact, Ikea is now the world's largest furniture retailer. It was founded in Sweden in 1943 by then-17-year-old Ingvar Kamprad, who, until his death in January 2018, was one of the richest people in the world, worth more than 40 billion dollars. The company's name is an acronym that consists of the initials of Ingvar Kamprad (name of founder), Elmtaryd (the farm where he grew up), and Agunnaryd (his hometown in Småland, southern Sweden.The company is known for its good value, eco-friendly, modernist designs, and for the simplicity of its products.

The annual harvest of timber in Sweden rose after World War II, from 34 million cubic meters in 1950 to 65 million cubic meters in 1971, then leveled off around 52 million cubic meters in the late 1980s. Besides providing raw materials for manufacturing products such as paper, pulp, wood-fiber boards, and a wide range of chemical extracts, the forests are an important source of fuel and building materials. Jobs in lumbering, the transport of timber, and the wood-processing industries employ about a quarter of a million workers. The most important timber industry is the production of planks and boards. Its output reached a peak in the early twentieth century and has remained fairly stable since the 1930s. Sawmills are located in the small ports of the Gulf of Bothnia, particularly at the mouths of the Ljungan, Indals, and Ångerman rivers. The port of Sundsvall boasts the largest concentration of wood-processing

THE SWEDISH ECONOMY

plants in the world. Sawmills located on the northern shore of Lake Vänern export cut timber through the city of Göteborg.

Timber is converted into pulp either by grinding (mechanical pulp) or by boiling and solution (chemical pulp). About 70 percent of Sweden's pulp is now produced by chemical processes. The pulp industry is concentrated mainly in the ports of southern Norrland, especially around Örnsköldsvik, and on the northern shore of Lake Vänern, where Skoghall is an important center. Sweden is one of a few countries who dominate the pulp industry. The most rapidly expanding branch of the industry produces sulfate pulp.

The paper industry is located mainly in central and southern Sweden, within reach of the shipping facilities of Göteborg and the national market in

ABOVE: *A sawmill at Bräkne-Hoby in Blekinge County.*

48

EUROPEAN COUNTRIES TODAY: SWEDEN

ABOVE: *A good deal of Sweden's lumber industry is located near the town of Örnsköldsvik on the North Sea coast.*

Stockholm for the newspaper and publishing industries. Norrköping and Halsta have important newsprint factories. Wrapping paper and cardboard are produced in the Göta valley and on the northern shore of Lake Vänern. Sweden is the fourth-ranking producer of newsprint in the world.

Mining
The mining of iron and copper has been important to Sweden since the Middle Ages. An enormously rich copper mine at Falun in the Bergslagen region was mined continuously for more than 650 years, until it was almost exhausted. In 2015, Sweden stood eleventh among the world producers of iron ore, of which it mined 25 million metric tons. Until the last quarter of the nineteenth century, the main iron mines were those in Bergslagen, but today the main source of

THE SWEDISH ECONOMY

iron ore is the remote northernmost part of Norrland. For the last century, the Norwegian ice-free port of Narvik has handled a majority of exports of Swedish ore. Swedish iron ores are extremely pure, with a phosphorus content of less than 0.3 percent. Bergslagen supplies most of the ore for the iron and steel manufacturing. Its most important mining center, Grängesberg, supplies the integrated iron and steel plant at Oxelösund on the Baltic coast.

Sweden is an important producer of copper. A new copper deposit was found in the early 1900s along the Skellefte River in Norrland. The main centers of copper mining are at Kristineberg, Boliden, and Adak, with some production still in Bergslagen. Zinc production, of which Sweden ranked tenth in the world in 2016, comes from a number of sites in both the north and south. Nickel, lead, silver, and gold are also mined in Sweden. Large uranium deposits supply the nation's nuclear-power industry.

ABOVE: *The vast copper mine at Falun is now a museum and World Heritage Site.*

EUROPEAN COUNTRIES TODAY: SWEDEN

The Economy of Sweden

Gross Domestic Product (GDP): $497 billion (2016 est.)
GDP Per Capita: $49,800 (2016 est.)
Industries: iron and steel, precision equipment (bearings, radio and telephone parts, armaments), wood pulp and paper products, processed foods, motor vehicles
Export Commodities: machinery 35%, motor vehicles, paper products, pulp and wood, iron and steel products, chemicals
Export Partners: Germany 10.6%, Norway 10.4%, US 7.3%, Denmark 7%, Finland 6.8%, UK 6%, Netherlands 5.4%, Belgium 4.7%, France 4.4% (2016)
Import Commodities: machinery, petroleum and petroleum products, chemicals, motor vehicles, iron and steel; foodstuffs, clothing
Import Partners: Germany 18.8%, Netherlands 8.2%, Norway 7.8%, Denmark 7.6%, China 5.6%, UK 5.2%, Belgium 4.6%, Finland 4.5%, France 4.1% (2016)
Currency: Swedish krona

Source: www.cia.gov 2017

Industry: The Mainstay of the Economy and Exports

Swedish manufacturing employs roughly 890,000 people. Metallurgy and engineering employed 48 percent of all manufacturing workers. The timber, pulp, and paper industries follow with 21 percent, the food and beverage industry with 9 percent, and the chemical industry with 8 percent.

The production of iron and steel is one of Sweden's vital industries. This industry is located mainly in Bergslagen. These modern iron and steel plants use the latest electrical smelting processes that eliminate some of the harmful

THE SWEDISH ECONOMY

ABOVE: *The old iron foundry at Bergslagen was founded in the 1300s. It is now a famous landmark.*

by-products of past manufacturing processes. The largest iron and steel works is at Domnarvet. Two large plants are also located near the coast, allowing for the easy import of coke and scrap metal, as well as the export of goods for engineering industries in other parts of Sweden and the port cities of northern Europe.

Engineering is the oldest and most highly developed manufacturing industry in Scandinavia. In Sweden, it accounts for about 40 percent of the total exports and produces a wide range of products, including machinery, tools, precision gauges, electrical generating equipment, ball bearings, automobiles, and military aircraft. Various engineering centers are scattered throughout the central lowlands between Stockholm and Göteborg. The plants are often set in regional clusters, particularly around the shores of Lake Mälaren and in the Göta valley. Malmö and the towns of southwestern Skåne are another important hub of engineering industries.

EUROPEAN COUNTRIES TODAY: SWEDEN

Sweden was a dominant force in shipbuilding for half a century until this industry went into rapid decline in the late 1970s. A glut of ships on the world market (particularly in oil tankers), two international recessions, and fierce competition from low-wage countries like South Korea and Brazil has caused the total output of Swedish shipyards to fall dramatically.

Agriculture

Agriculture has declined dramatically in importance in Sweden during the twentieth century. A basic feature of Swedish farming today is the widespread abandonment of land and the concentration of agriculture in the most favorable areas of the country. As small farms become deserted as their owners grow old and die, the government has intervened to compel the amalgamation of the property into larger units. Consequently the number of small, privately owned farms has declined significantly since the 1950s.

Although only about 2 percent of the labor force held agricultural jobs in 2014, compared with 29 percent in 1940, agricultural output has not declined. In fact, output has greatly increased, despite the reduced area of farmland, because of the impact of modern technology. Field drains, striking success in plant breeding for northern latitudes, widespread use of fertilizers, cooperatives for marketing agricultural commodities, and dissemination of technical information on farming have all contributed to increased harvests.

As in the other Scandinavian countries, the principal agricultural activity in Sweden is raising livestock. Because of the importance of livestock, three-quarters of the land under cultivation is devoted to fodder crops. More than half of this area is devoted to growing rotation grass, a fast growing combination of rye grass, timothy, and clover. Most of this grass is converted into hay for the indoor feeding of livestock in winter, which lasts from five to seven months. Cereals are the second-most important crop. The main wheat-producing areas are the central lowlands and Skåne, though spring wheat is grown at favorable sites in Norrland's valleys as far north as the Arctic Circle. Rye and oats grow extensively on the western coastal plains. Barley is an important fodder crop in southwest Skåne.

THE SWEDISH ECONOMY

the world, the recession soon spread from the United States around the globe. As a result, the EU's economy also entered a recession—and so did Sweden.

From the early 1990s until 2008, Sweden had enjoyed a long period of economic strength that was fueled by strong exports and a rising demand within the country for goods and services. At the end of 2008, however, Sweden entered the recession that the rest of the world was already experiencing. Much of the Swedish economy was dependent on exporting cars, construction equipment, and telecommunication services—but now people and companies in the rest of the world no longer had as much money to buy these goods and services. Exports dropped, and Swedish companies were forced to slow down. During 2009, the gross domestic product (GDP) dropped by nearly 5 percent. But the Swedish economy bounced back faster than anyone expected it would. By 2010, GDP had grown by 5.5 percent, regaining the ground it had lost in 2009. More recent figures show that Sweden's economy experienced modest growth between 2014 and 2016, with real GDP growth above 2 percent. However, the country has continued to struggle with deflationary pressure.

Sweden has a strong, stable government that rules many areas of Swedish life, and the economy is no exception. Thanks to Swedish government policies, the Swedish national budget is always kept balanced. (The situation in the United States has been far different!) The Swedish budget process sets spending ceilings; these are promises that the government makes to its people—and keeps. This meant that when the economic crisis began in 2008, Sweden went in with a budget surplus. This was a key factor that allowed Sweden to ride out the crisis better than most of the world's other countries.

Figures for the third-quarter of 2017 showed a period of robust economic activity. Quarter-on-quarter GDP growth came in significantly above the EU average, boosted by surging fixed investment. This success has been helped by the goverment targeting job creation, maintaining the welfare state, promoting exports, and tackling climate change. A series of additional reforms, such as lowering taxes on low- and middle-income earners, has also helped the economy.

One of the ways Sweden stimulates growth and raises revenue is through the sale of public assets. Over the last 10 years, the government has sold vast

EUROPEAN COUNTRIES TODAY: SWEDEN

ABOVE: Headquarters of Swedish bank Svenska Handelsbanken, in Stockholm.

THE SWEDISH ECONOMY

state assets, including the Swedish OMX Stock Exchange to Borse Dubai/Nasdaq for $318 million. Additionally, the government sold most of its 946 drugstores and eliminated its monopoly on pharmacies. The government also approved the sale of Svensk Bilprovning (the Swedish Motor Vehicle Inspection Company).

The Swedish banking sector is made up of four large companies that account for about 80 percent of all banking activity in Sweden. The Swedish banks are heavily invested in the Baltic countries, which were some of the countries hardest hit during the financial crisis. Swedish banks suffered as a result; the

ABOVE: *Korsgatan is a busy shopping street in Göteborg.*

EUROPEAN COUNTRIES TODAY: SWEDEN

government responded with a bank support package in 2008 that included guarantees for new debt insurance, increased deposit insurance, and a fund that would provide up to $6 billion in funds to be injected into vital organizations. Today, Sweden's economy is doing well, thanks in part to investments designed to address a housing shortage and care for a record number of immigrants from war-torn countries like Syria and Iraq. The central bank, for its part, has helped fuel private consumption by cutting interest rates deep below zero and buying bonds. A high-tech economy and a comprehensive system of welfare benefits give Sweden one of the highest standards of living in the world, allowing its people and culture to thrive.

Text-Dependent Questions

1. Which natural resources can be found in Sweden?

2. How long has iron and copper mining been important to Sweden?

3. How do living standards in Sweden compare with other countries?

Research Project

Write a brief report on Sweden's most important industries.

Words to Understand

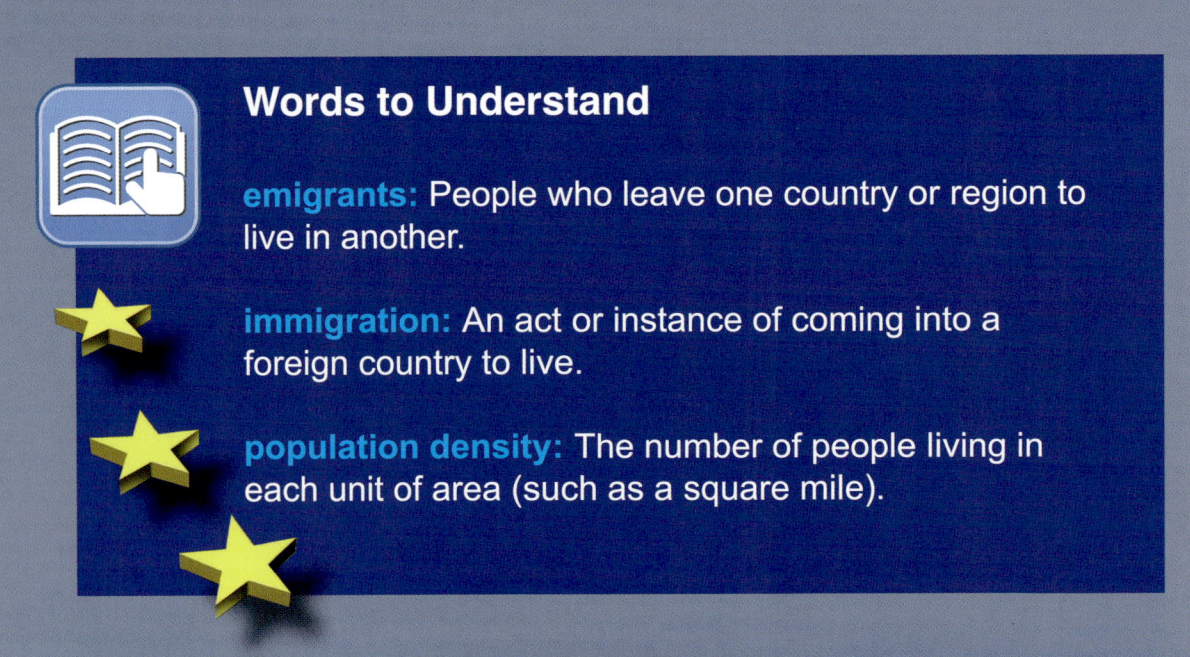

emigrants: People who leave one country or region to live in another.

immigration: An act or instance of coming into a foreign country to live.

population density: The number of people living in each unit of area (such as a square mile).

BELOW: The Öresundsbron links Copenhagen in Denmark with Malmö in Sweden.

Chapter Four
CITIZENS OF SWEDEN: PEOPLE, CUSTOMS & CULTURE

The population of Sweden was estimated at 9,960,487 in 2017. This gives the country an overall **population density** of 63 persons per square mile (24 per sq. km). Although Sweden as a whole is sparsely populated, regional population densities can vary greatly. The great majority of the population lives in the southern third of Sweden, especially in the central lowlands, the plains of Skåne, and coastal areas. Population is densest around the cities of

ABOVE: In Sweden, Midsummer's Eve is one of the most important days of the year, rivaling Christmas with its festive spirit and traditions. Traditionally, Midsummer Eve is celebrated on June 24, the feast day of St. John the Baptist, but the holiday has its roots in a pre-Christian solstice festival.

CITIZENS OF SWEDEN: PEOPLE, CUSTOMS & CULTURE

ABOVE: *Swedes from all religious and cultural backgrounds participate in National Day celebrations, which takes place every year on June 6.*

Stockholm, Göteborg, and Malmö. Large areas of the north are sparsely inhabited. Sweden is also highly urbanized, with more than 80 percent of Swedes living in the nation's cities.

Ethnically, Sweden consists mainly of Scandinavians of Germanic descent. Due to a dramatic increase in **immigration**, Sweden's ethnic diversity has grown rapidly in recent decades. For many years, Sweden was a nation of **emigrants**. From 1860 to World War I, more than one million Swedes left the nation, mainly for the United States. Emigration declined significantly after 1930, as the nation grew more prosperous. Following World War II, Sweden welcomed many refugees and displaced people. Since then, immigration has accounted for nearly half of Sweden's population growth. Today, approximately

EUROPEAN COUNTRIES TODAY: SWEDEN

ABOVE: *Sami women in traditional dress in Lapland. The Sami tend to mainly live in the north, though some now live in the south.*

CITIZENS OF SWEDEN: PEOPLE, CUSTOMS & CULTURE

20 percent of the population are immigrants or have at least one foreign-born parent. Many of these immigrants have come to Sweden as political refugees.

The largest immigrant groups in Sweden are from neighboring Scandinavian countries. About 17,000 ethnic Sami live mainly in the far north, although in recent decades many Sami have migrated south, mainly to Stockholm. Sweden is also home to large numbers of immigrants who fled the conflict in the former Yugoslavia, especially Serbia and Montenegro and Bosnia and Herzegovina. In fact, only Germany has received more refugees from that region. Other important immigrant groups include people from Iran, Iraq, Hungary, Syria, Turkey, and Poland.

ABOVE: Zlatan Ibrahimović is a famous Swedish footballer. He was born in Malmö in Sweden. Both his parents were immigrants who moved to Sweden in the 1970s. His father is a Bosnian Muslim and his mother a Croatian Catholic.

EUROPEAN COUNTRIES TODAY: SWEDEN

Educational Video

Education in Sweden from age 1 to adulthood.

Education

In Sweden, *förskola* (preschool) is provided for children ages one to six. Play is an important element of preschool. Children may attend at any age between 1 and 6 but it is not compulsory. All children must attend comprehensive school from about the age of 7 to 15. If the student achieves good grades they may attend upper secondary from the ages of 16 to 20. Students who do not achieve sufficient grades will attend a special-needs upper-secondary school.

After completing secondary school, students may go on to adult education such as university.

Religion

The Swedish constitution guarantees freedom of religion. Approximately 80 percent of the population belongs to the Church of Sweden. It is possible to leave the Church of Sweden, and an increasing number of people do. In 1999, the Church of Sweden and the state separated, and as a result more than twice as many people left the Church in that year as in the previous years.

While weekly services in Christian houses of worship are usually poorly attended, a large number of people observe major festivals of the Church and prefer a religious ceremony to mark the turning points of life. Approximately 70 percent of children are baptized, 40 percent of those eligible are confirmed, and 90 percent of funeral services are performed under the auspices of the Church

CITIZENS OF SWEDEN: PEOPLE, CUSTOMS & CULTURE

of Sweden. Approximately 60 percent of couples marrying choose a Church of Sweden ceremony. There are several smaller Christian-faith communities in Sweden as well. The Roman Catholic Church and the Russian Orthodox Church are represented. Several small churches are offshoots of nineteenth-century revival movements in the Church of Sweden. Others, such as the Baptist Union of Sweden and the Methodist Church of Sweden, trace their roots to British and North American protestant movements.

ABOVE: *This medieval Lutheran church is situated on a small island called Fårö, near the larger island of Gotland. In the church cemetery is the grave of film-maker Ingmar Bergman and his wife Ingrid von Rosen. They were buried there together in 2007.*

EUROPEAN COUNTRIES TODAY: SWEDEN

ABOVE: *The Islamic Center in Malmö comprises a school and a mosque. It was inaugurated in 1984.*

The Jewish community has 10,000 active, practicing members; however, the total number of Jews living in the country is estimated to be approximately 20,000. The Muslim community has approximately 350,000 members, of whom around 100,000 are active.

CITIZENS OF SWEDEN: PEOPLE, CUSTOMS & CULTURE

Food and Drink

Swedish food is usually simple and satisfying, and nowadays also healthy. In the last few decades immigrants from all over the world have enriched Swedish food culture with a host of exciting dishes. Foreign fast food, for example, has become an inseparable part of Swedish youth culture.

The feature of Swedish cuisine most familiar to foreigners is the *smörgåsbord.* The word *smörgås* means "open sandwich," and *bord* is the Swedish word for "table," but a smörgåsbord is not a table full of sandwiches. Instead, this specialty consists of a number of small dishes, from which you can take your pick. A typical smörgåsbord usually contains a number of herring dishes, Swedish meatballs, salmon, pies, salads, "Jansson's temptation" (sliced

Swedish Meatballs

Makes 4 servings

Ingredients
Meatballs:
1 egg
1 cup soft breadcrumbs
1 teaspoon brown sugar
½ teaspoon salt
¼ teaspoon each: pepper, ginger, ground cloves, nutmeg, cinnamon
½ cup milk
cooking oil

Sour Cream Sauce:
2 tablespoons butter
2 tablespoons flour
1 cup beef broth
½ teaspoon salt
dash cayenne pepper
½ teaspoon Worcestershire sauce
1 cup dairy sour cream, room temperature

Directions
Mix thoroughly all of the ingredients for the meatballs except the oil. Form into 12

meatballs. Fry in hot oil, about 1-inch deep, until fully cooked, turning only once. Drain completely on paper towels.

Pour all excess oil from frying pan. Add the butter to the pan, and stir in the flour. Cook until bubbly; do not let it brown. Add broth, salt, cayenne pepper, and Worcestershire sauce; cook, stirring until thickened (the sauce will not reach its full thickness until it boils). Empty sour cream into a large bowl. Add a small amount of the sauce to the sour cream and stir. Gradually add the rest of the sauce, stirring constantly. Fold meatballs into the sauce. Spoon into a chafing dish, stainless steel, or enamel pan. Heat gently to serving temperature. Serve with boiled potatoes or hot noodles. Garnish with minced parsley.

Lussekatter (Lucia Buns)
This classic Swedish pasty is traditionally served on St. Lucia Day (December 13).

Yields 12 buns

Ingredients
⅓ cup milk
¼ cup butter
¼ cup warm water
1 yeast package
¼ cup sugar
2 eggs
½ teaspoon salt
¼ teaspoon saffron
2 ¾ cups flour
vegetable oil
1 tablespoon water
raisins

Directions
Combine the milk and butter in a small saucepan, and heat until the butter melts.

Mix the warm water and yeast in a large bowl. Add the warm milk mixture. Add one egg, sugar, salt, and saffron. Add 1 ½ cups of flour and mix well. Gradually add more flour until the dough is stiff. Knead the dough on a floured surface for 5 to 10 minutes. Coat a large bowl with cooking oil and put in the dough. Cover with a towel and let the dough rise in a warm location until it has doubled in size.

After the dough has doubled, punch it down. Divide it into 12 sections, rolling each section into a rope. Roll the ends in opposite directions until they meet in the middle (see picture). Carefully place the buns on a greased cookie sheet, cover, and let rise until they are doubled in size.

When ready to bake, preheat the oven to 350°F. In a small dish, beat an egg with the water. Using a pastry brush, lightly brush the buns with egg wash. Decorate with raisins. Bake for 15 to 20 minutes, or until golden brown.

CITIZENS OF SWEDEN: PEOPLE, CUSTOMS & CULTURE

ABOVE: *A traditional food market in central Stockholm*

herring, potatoes, and onions baked in cream), eggs, bread, and some kind of potato dish. Smörgåsbord was originally served in the eighteenth century as an appetizer before the main course. Today, however, it has become a meal in itself. Few people ask for more after having tried everything on a smörgåsbord!

Refugees in Sweden

When people flee their home country to escape war, famine, or oppression, they are known as refugees. Sweden accepts nearly 2,000 political refugees each year. The Swedish government is concerned, however, that the rest of the EU is not doing its share. The government has made this official statement regarding refugees:

  "*Sweden must take its share of the responsibility for the international protection of refugees. An important part of this responsibility is to provide protection—through resettlement in Sweden—for people fleeing in a third*

EUROPEAN COUNTRIES TODAY: SWEDEN

ABBA

Formed in 1972, ABBA is a world-famous Swedish pop group, formed by members Agnetha Fältskog, Björn Ulvaeus, Benny Andersson, and Anni-Frid Lyngstad. The group's name was invented by combining the first letter of each band members' names. ABBA is one of the most commercially successful acts in the history of popular music and over the decades has topped the charts worldwide. ABBA's first major success was winning the Eurovision Song Contest for Sweden in 1974, in the United Kindgom. This victory was Sweden's first triumph in the contest and even after all those years since, ABBA are still the most successful group to have ever taken part in the competition.

ABBA is one of the best-selling music groups of all time. ABBA was the first group from a non-English-speaking country to achieve consistent success in the charts of English-speaking countries, including the United Kingdom, Ireland, Canada, Australia, New Zealand, South Africa, and the United States.

The band officially split 1982, however there have been reunions 1986 and 2008. Today, the band is still working on various projects, uniting periodically for specialist ventures.

https://en.wikipedia.org/wiki/ABBA

CITIZENS OF SWEDEN: PEOPLE, CUSTOMS & CULTURE

country who do not have access to any other permanent solution. Sweden is to engage in constructive cooperation with the UN Refugee Agency (UNHCR) and to have a humane refugee policy, as well as be a place of refuge for people fleeing persecution and oppression. The possibility of seeking asylum must be safeguarded and the trend in Europe towards more closed borders must be opposed. One of the Government's primary objectives in the area of migration is common asylum rules for countries in the EU. All EU Member States must share the responsibility for offering protection to refugees. If Sweden has to shoulder a disproportionate share of the responsibility for refugee situations around the world in relation to comparable countries, this will eventually raise questions about the sustainability of our asylum system."

ABOVE: *Swedish military preparing to salute the birth of Prince Oscar of Sweden in 2016.*

EUROPEAN COUNTRIES TODAY: SWEDEN

Militarity Neutrality

Although Sweden is a full member of the EU, today it still keeps its policy of military neutrality. (In other words, during a war or military conflict, Sweden will not take sides or become involved.) This was a nonnegotiable Swedish condition during its membership process; it was simply too important to how Sweden views itself as a nation for its citizens to consider it giving up! However, Sweden does fully support the EU's conflict-prevention efforts, as well as its work to manage civil and military crises. Sweden is also willing to participate in European peacekeeping activities and humanitarian efforts.

Text-Dependent Questions

1. Where do most people live in Sweden?

2. How may ethnic Sami live in Sweden?

3. What is the predominant religion in Sweden?

Research Project

Write a one-page biography on Ingmar Bergman or Alfred Nobel.

Words to Understand

information technology: The technology involving the development, maintenance, and use of computers and software for the processing and distribution of information.

populated: Inhabited or lived in.

urban: Related to a city or town.

BELOW: A Christmas market in Stortorget, a public square in Gamla Stan (Old Town), Stockholm.

Chapter Five
THE FAMOUS CITIES OF SWEDEN

Today's Sweden is heavily urbanized, with more than 80 percent of the nation's people living in and around **urban** areas. As a result, the rest of Sweden is thinly **populated**, giving the country one of the lowest population densities in Europe. Sweden's three largest and most important cities are Stockholm, the capital; Göteborg; and Malmö. Other major cities include Uppsala, Linköping, Örebro, Norrköping, and Västerås.

Stockholm: The Capital

Stockholm has a population of 942,370. The city is often compared to Venice because of its scenic bridges and waterways and its historic architecture. Located in east-central Sweden, the city is built on about twenty islands and a narrow strip of land between Lake Mälaren and the Baltic Sea. Stockholm is famous for its historic quarter, the Old Town (Gamla Stan), located on three central islands in the city's harbor. Old Town is home to the magnificent Royal Palace, Stockholm's City Hall (the Stadthuset), and the Great Church, a part of which dates to the

ABOVE: *The Stockholm City Hall is one of Sweden's most famous buildings, and one of the capital's most visited tourist attractions.*

THE FAMOUS CITIES OF SWEDEN

Educational Video

A travel guide to Stockholm's famous sights.

thirteenth century. Stockholm is Sweden's financial, commercial, cultural, and administrative center.

Göteborg

Göteborg (Gothenburg), Sweden's second-largest city, is located on the Kattegat, the strait separating Sweden from Denmark. The city has a tremendous harbor, the largest in Scandinavia, and is the country's leading port. Göteborg is a critical transportation hub on the Göta Canal, and is home to a large international airport. Despite being hard-hit by the decline of the Swedish shipbuilding industry, Göteborg remains an important industrial city, with factories producing automobiles, automobile parts, and telecommunications equipment. It is also a center for banking and financial services, medical research and pharmaceuticals, and **information technology**. The city also boasts the famous Göteborg Botanical Garden and Liseberg, the largest amusement park in Scandinavia and one of Sweden's most popular tourist attractions.

Malmö

Malmö is Sweden's third-largest city. It is home to one of Sweden's major ports and is also a rail, air, and highway hub. Malmö is the headquarters of Sweden's pharmaceuticals industry, and its modern fiber optic cable networks support a

EUROPEAN COUNTRIES TODAY: SWEDEN

ABOVE: *Göteborg largely grew around its many waterways. Today, visitors can see the city's sights by boat.*

77

THE FAMOUS CITIES OF SWEDEN

Öresundsbron and Drogden Tunnel

The Öresundsbron is the longest combined road and rail bridge and tunnel in Europe and connects two major metropolitan areas: Copenhagen, the Danish capital city, and the Swedish city of Malmö. The bridge makes it possible to travel between Sweden and Denmark in just fifteen minutes. It connects the road and rail networks of the Scandinavian Peninsula with those of Central and Western Europe. A data cable connected to the bridge connects internet data transmission between Central Europe and other Scandinavian countries.

EUROPEAN COUNTRIES TODAY: SWEDEN

vigorous information technology sector. In 2000, an important bridge and tunnel opened, connecting Malmö with Copenhagen, Denmark. Copenhagen, once accessible only by air or sea, is located just fifteen miles (24 kilometers) across Öresund Strait. The bridge, called Öresundsbron, makes it possible to travel between Sweden and Denmark in just fifteen minutes.

ABOVE: The historic Stortorget square in Malmö.

THE FAMOUS CITIES OF SWEDEN

ABOVE: *Two of Uppsala's main landmarks—the cathedral (Uppsala domkyrka) and the county museum (Upplands museet).*

Uppsala

Uppsala is Sweden's fourth-largest city. Perhaps best known for its university, founded in the fifteenth century, the city also offers visitors beautiful surroundings, a lively cultural scene, and a wealth of historic architecture. Today, Uppsala is a vibrant industrial and commercial city. At Uppsala University, extensive research is carried out in a number of fields to promote the development of industry, commerce, and entrepreneurship. Uppsala is also Scandinavia's leading medical center. The country's only pharmacy and veterinary medicine colleges can be found here.

EUROPEAN COUNTRIES TODAY: SWEDEN

ABOVE: *The sixteenth-century Royal Uppsala Castle is in the historic city of Uppsala. The castle has played a major role in the history of Sweden.*

THE FAMOUS CITIES OF SWEDEN

ABOVE: *Linköping has an ancient past. Today, the city is known for its university and its high-technology industries.*

EUROPEAN COUNTRIES TODAY: SWEDEN

Linköping

Linköping, Sweden's fifth-largest city, has an ancient history as county town, as a military city, and as a center of learning. Historic Linköping Castle now accommodates the home of the county governor. The Castle and Cathedral Museum is a prominent tourist attraction. Next to the castle and the cathedral is the Katedralskolan, which was the first school in Linköping. The city is now recognized as an important city of learning. Today, Linköping is a dynamic university town and center of commerce. Economic development began to expand when Saab located its aircraft manufacturing facilities here in 1937.

Text Dependent Questions

1. What is the population of Stockholm?

2. What is Sweden's second-largest city?

3. When was Uppsala University founded?

Research Project

Create a map of Sweden and clearly indicate all of Sweden's major cities.

Words to Understand

market economy: An economy in which most goods and services are produced and distributed through free markets.

philosophy: A set of ideas about how to do something or how to live.

tax burden: The amount of income, property, or sales tax levied on an individual or business.

BELOW: Swedes benefit from a generous welfare system. Benefits include free childcare, health care, and pensions.

Chapter Six
A BRIGHT FUTURE FOR SWEDEN

Social Welfare

Home to the world's highest **tax burden**, Sweden has created what is often called the world's most generous social welfare system, with such elements as virtually free (that is, tax-financed) education, child care, health care, pensions, elder care, social services, and various other social security systems.

Although Sweden has always had a solid **market economy**, the Social Democratic Party that ran the government for most of the twentieth century borrowed many ideas from socialism. Swedish wealth has been redistributed among the population to a greater extent than in perhaps any other country. "From each according to ability, to each according to needs" is the basic **philosophy** of socialism, which guarantees all people economic security in all stages of life.

The Swedish welfare state, known in Sweden as the "home of the people," is a unique experiment in social engineering that has attracted attention worldwide. In recent decades, however, the Swedish welfare state has been

ABOVE: Swedish and EU flags.

85

A BRIGHT FUTURE FOR SWEDEN

ABOVE: Wind power turbines along the coast of Halland County in western Sweden.

under heavy pressures. Today, the country's social security systems are financially burdened and are struggling with serious structural problems. The recent flood of poor refugees and immigrants has increased the drain on the welfare system. Yet the main features of the Swedish welfare state, with its guaranteed and publicly financed safety net for the entire population, so far remain largely unchanged.

The Environment

The safety of the planet's future is of primary importance to Swedes. They understand that without the Earth, no economy would last long; if the Earth

EUROPEAN COUNTRIES TODAY: SWEDEN

suffers, we will all suffer too. Because of this strong prevailing philosophy, the Swedish Parliament is aiming to solve all the country's major environmental problems within a single generation. The goal is to create a truly sustainable society. To do this, it has committed to fifteen objectives that are based on the following five fundamental principles:

- promotion of human health
- preservation of biological diversity
- preservation of cultural heritage assets
- preservation of long-term production capacity of ecosystems
- wise management of natural resources

The fifteen objectives are:
1. Reduced climate impact
2. Clean air
3. Natural acidification only
4. A non-toxic environment
5. A protective ozone layer
6. A safe radiation environment
7. Zero eutrophication
8. Flourishing lakes and streams
9. Good-quality groundwater
10. A balanced marine environment
11. Flourishing coastal areas and archipelagos (islands)
12. Thriving wetlands
13. Sustainable forests
14. A varied agricultural landscape
15. A magnificent mountain landscape

By making this commitment, Sweden is truly setting an example for the entire world.

Like any nation, Sweden faces many problems. But Sweden is determined to overcome them all!

A BRIGHT FUTURE FOR SWEDEN

ABOVE: H&M is a Swedish clothing company that has stores all over the world. The chain is important to Sweden's economy.

EUROPEAN COUNTRIES TODAY: SWEDEN

It's easy to do business in Sweden

According to the World Economic Forum, it's really easy to do business in Sweden. So much so that it now ranks number four on the *Forbes* annual list of the Best Countries for Business. Compare that to economic powerhouse the US, which is in twelfth place.

Fifteen years ago, Sweden ranked much lower, but since then it has embarked upon a number of initiatives that have propelled it to the top. "Over the past two decades the country has undergone a transformation built on deregulation and budget self-restraint with cuts to Sweden's welfare state," says *Forbes*. It is also home to plenty of tech innovation and to "some of the most venerable, well-known brands in the world, including Volvo, Electrolux, Ericsson, IKEA, and H&M."

Text Dependent Questions

1. What is the major political party in Sweden?

2. What are the main elements of the Swedish welfare system?

3. How many environmental objectives does the Swedish government have?

Research Project

Write a brief report on the Swedish welfare system.

CHRONOLOGY

9000 BCE	Petroglyphs are carved by Sweden's earliest human inhabitants.
98 CE	The Roman historian Tacitus describes a tribe of peoples called the Suiones, now recognized as Swedes.
793	Vikings emerge as the dominant power in Sweden.
1066	King Harald is defeated while invading England, marking the end of the Viking Age.
1397	Sweden joins Denmark under the Kalmar Union.
1523	The Kalmar Union is dissolved.
1658	The Swedish Empire is at the height of its power.
1718	Sweden loses the Great Northern War.
1772	King Gustav reestablishes absolute monarchy.
1809	Adoption of a new constitution.
1905	Official separation of Norway.
1914	World War I begins. Sweden remains neutral.
1917	Constitutional monarchy founded on parliamentary democracy.
1921	Universal suffrage for men and women.
1939	World War II begins. Sweden remains neutral.
1946	Sweden joins the United Nations.
1960	Sweden becomes a founding member of the European Free Trade Association.
1992	European Economic Area agreement is signed
1993	Sweden begins accession negotiations with the EU.
1995	Sweden joins the EU.
2008	Worldwide recession begins.
2009	Sweden's GDP decreases by nearly 5 percent.
2010	Sweden's economy bounces back from the recession.
2012	Sweden's opposition Social Democrat Party leader Håkan Juholt resigns.
2014	Sweden announces plans to boost annual defence spend by 5.5bn kronor.
2014	Stefan Löfven becomes premier following parliamentary elections.
2017	In Stockholm, a hijacked lorry was deliberately driven into crowds along Drottninggatan (Queen Street) before being crashed through the corner a department store. Five people were killed and fourteen others were seriously injured.

FURTHER READING & INTERNET RESOURCES

Further Reading

Johansson, Ulf. Neppenstrom, Mona. Sandell Kaj. *DK Eyewitness Travel Guide: Sweden.* London: DK, 2017.

Mason, David S. *A Concise History of Modern Europe: Liberty, Equality, Solidarity.* London: Rowman & Littlefield, 2015.

McCormick, John. *Understanding the European Union: A Concise Introduction.* London: Palgrave Macmillan, 2017.

Walker, Benedict. McLachlan, Craig. Ohlsen, Becky. *Lonely Planet Sweden (Travel Guide).* London: Lonely Planet Publications, 2018.

Internet Resources

Sweden Travel Information and Travel Guide
https://www.lonelyplanet.com/sweden

Official Site of Sweden
https://sweden.se

Sweden: Country Profile
http://www.bbc.co.uk/news/world-europe-17955808

Sweden: CIA World Factbook
https://www.cia.gov/library/publications/the-world-factbook/geos/sw.html

The Official Website of the European Union
europa.eu/index_en.htm

Publisher's note:
The websites listed on this page were active at the time of publication. The publisher is not responsible for websites that have changed their addressees or discontinued operation since the date of publication. The publisher will review and update the website list upon each reprint.

INDEX

A
ABBA, 71
Adak, 50
Adils, King, 27
Agriculture, 16, 33, 44, 45, 53–54
Agunnaryd, 47
Åland Islands, 38
Albert, King, 30
Ale's Stones, 24
Allies, 37–38
Andersson, Benny, 71
Ångermanälven river, 17
Ångerman river, 47
Animals, 21, 22–23
Arctic Circle, 11, 14, 19, 20, 53
Area, 7
Aun, King, 27
Australia, 71
Austria, 35
Axis Powers, 37

B
Baltic Sea, 7, 13, 16, 17, 18, 19, 23
Banking, 58, 59
Baptists, 9
Baptist Union of Sweden, 66
Barley, 44, 53
Beach of Grenen, 13
Belgium, 35, 43, 51
Beowulf, 26
Bergman, Ingmar, 66
Bergslagen, 49, 50, 52
Berlin, 39
Birth rate, 9
Björn, King, 28
Black Sea, 27
Blekinge County, 48
Boliden, 50
Borders, 7, 13
Borse Dubai/Nasdaq, 58
Bosnia and Herzegovina, 64
Bräkne-Hoby, 48
Brazil, 53
Brofjordan, 55

Brussels, 42, 43
Buddhism, 9

C
Canada, 71
Capital, 11
Carl XVI Gustav, King, 39
Castle and Cathedral Museum, 83
Charles
    King, 33
    VIII, King, 30
China, 51
Christian
    I, King, 31
    II, King, 31
    III, King, 30
Christianization, 28–30
Christmas, 61, 74
Church of Sweden, 9, 29, 32, 65–66
Cities, 75–83
Climate, 7, 19–21
Conservative Party, 33
Constantinople, 27
Cooperatives, 46
Copenhagen, 60, 78, 79
Copper, 50
Cormorant, 21
Coup d'état, 33
Cranach, Lucas, 32
Currency, 51

D
Dalälven river, 17
Daylight hours, 44
Death rate, 9
Denmark, 8, 13, 27, 29, 30, 32, 38, 51, 60, 76, 78, 79
Domnarvet, 52
Drogden Tunnel, 78

E
Economy, 33, 45–59, 51
    budget, 56
    current, 55, 57–59

    depression, 35
    growth, 56
    market economy, 85
    recession, 56
Education, 65
Egil, King, 27
Electrolux, 89
Elevation, 7
Elmtaryd, 47
Emigrants, 62
Energy, 54–55
Engineering, 52
England, 33
    invasion of, 28
Entry of King Gustav Vasa of Sweden into Stockholm, The (Larsson), 31
Environment, 86–87
    fundamental principles, 87
    objectives, 87
Ericsson, 89
Eric the Victorious, 28
Erik, King, 28
Estonia, 32, 38
Ethnic groups, 9, 62, 64
European
    Coal and Steel Community, 43
    Community, 43
    Economic Community, 43
European Union (EU), 8, 23, 41, 70, 72, 73
    autonomy, 42, 43
    flag, 85
    formation, 42–43
    members, 42, 43
    Parliament Building, 42, 43
    single market, 43
Eurovision Song Contest, 71
Exporta, 45, 52, 56
Exports, 51

F
Fältsborg, Agnetha, 71
Falun, 49, 50
Fårö, 66

INDEX

Faroe Island, 38
Ferdinand, Archduke, 35
Fertility rate, 9
Feudal system, 29
Finland, 7, 9, 13, 51
Finnish
 language, 9
 people, 9
Fish, 23
Fjällbacka, 20
Flag, 8, 85
Fog, 20
Food and drink, 68–70
Forbes, 89
Forestry, 46–49
Forests, 8, 14, 15, 22, 45. *See also* Forestry
Forkbeard, King Svein, 27
Förskola (preschool), *65*
France, 35, 37, 42, 43, 51
Furniture, 47
Future, 85–89

G

Gamla
 Stan (Old Town), 8, 10, 40, 74, 75
 Uppsala, 27
Geography, 7
 and landscape, 11–24
Germanic descent, 62
Germany, 32, 35, 37–38, 51
Glaciers, 11
Göta
 Canal, 18, 76
 valley, 49, 52
Götaland (Land of the Goths), 13, 15
Göteborg, 20, 48, 52, 55, 58, 62, 75, 76, 77
 Botanical Garden, 76
Gotland, 12, 13, 16, 22, 66
Government, 25–43, 56
 asset sales, 56
Grängesberg, 49–50
Great

Britain, 35, 37
Church, 75–76
Depression, 35
Northern War, 32
Greenland, 38
Gross domestic product (GDP), 51, 56
 per capita, 51
Gulf
 of Bothnia, 7, 11, 13, 17, 20, 47
 Stream, 19
Gustav
 III, King, 33, 37
 Vasa, King, 31

H

Habitation, signs of, 25
Halland County, 85
Halsta, 49
Hansson, Per Albin, 34
Harald, 28
Hazards, 7
Helsingborg, 55
History, 25–43
Hitler, Adolph, 35, 37
Hjälmaren lake, 18
H&M, 88, 89
Höga Kusten (High Coast Bridge), 17
Holsteins, 30–31
Hydroelectric power, 17, 45, 54, 55

I

Ibrahimovíc, Zlatan, 64
Ice
 age, 11
 floes, 7, 19
Iceland, 38
IKEA, 47, 89
Immigration, 33, 62, 64, 85
Imports, 51
Indals river, 47
Industrialization, 33
Industries, 51

Infant mortality rate, 9
Information technology, 76
Ingria, 32
Iran, 9
Iraq, 9, 59
Ireland, 71
Iron, 51, 52
 Age, 25–28
 ore, 49–50
Islam, 9
Islamic Center, 67
Islands, 13, 16
Italy, 37, 43

J

Jämtland, 25
Japan, 37
Jordanes, 26
Judaism, 9, 67

K

Kalmar Union, 30–31
Kamprad, Ingvar, 47
Karlshamn, 55
Kåseberga, 24
Katedralskolan, 83
Kattegat, 7, 76
 Sea, 13
 strait, 13
Kebnekaise, 7, 14
Kiruna, 15
Korsgatan, 58
Kristiansad, 7
Kristineberg, 50
Krona, 51

L

Labor reform, 35
Läckö Castle, 18
Lake Hammarsjon, 7
Lakes, 11, 15, 18, 23, 46
Lake Vänern, 18
Language, 9
Lapland, 15, 63
Larsson, Carl, 31
Latvia, 38

93

INDEX

Liberal Party, 33
Lidköping, 18
Life expectancy, 9
Linköping, 82, 83
    Castle, 83
Liseberg, 76
Literacy rate, 9
Lithuania, 38
Livestock, 53
Livonia, 32
Ljungan river, 47
Location, 7
Löfven, Stefan, 41
Longships, 27
Luleå, 55
Lumber, 17, 45, 46–49, 51
Lussekatter (Lucia Buns), 60
Luther, Martin, 31
Lutheranism, 32
Lutherans, 9
Luxembourg, 43
Lyngstad, Anni-Frid, 71

M

Maastricht Treaty, 43
Magnus
    King, 28
    Ladulås, King, 29
Mälaren lake, 18, 52, 75
Malmö, 52, 55, 60, 62, 64, 67, 75, 76, 78, 79
Manufacturing, 51
Map, 6
Margaret I, Queen, 29, 30
Martin Luther (Cranach the Elder), 32
Meänkieli language, 9
Merger Treaty, 43
Methodist Church of Sweden, 66
Midsummer's Eve, 61
Migration rate, 9
Military, 35, 72
    neutrality, 73
    service, 33
Mining, 15, 49–50

Modernization, 33, 35
Monarchy, 40
    limited, 33
Monopolies, trade, 33
Montenegro, 64
Mountains, 14
Mount Kebne, 14

N

Napoleonic Wars, 33
Narvik, 50
National Day, 62
Nazi Party, 35
Netherlands, 43, 51
Neutrality, 34, 35, 37, 41
    armed, 37–38
    military, 73
Newsprint, 49
New Zealand, 71
Nordic Council, 38
Norrköping, 49
Norrland (Northland), 13, 14, 17, 50, 53, 55
North
    Atlantic Ocean, 19
    Sea, 13, 23, 49
Norway, 7, 13, 27, 29, 30, 33, 38, 51
Novgorod, 27
Nuclear power, 54
Nyköping, 25

O

Odin, 28
Öland, 13, 16, 22
Old
    Town. *See* Gamla Stan (Old Town)
    Uppsala (Gamla Uppsala), 27
Olof, 29
Olof, King, 28
OMX Stock Exchange, 58
Öresundsbron, 60, 78, 79
Öresund strait, 13
Örnsköldsvik, 49

Orthodox Christian, 9
Oscar, Prince, 72
Österlen, 24
Oxelösund, 50

P

Paper industry, 48
Paris, 35
Parliament, 87
Peace of Westphalia, 32
People, 9, 61–74
Petroglyphs, 25
Phocine distemper virus (PDV), 23
Piteå, 20
Plants, 21–22
Poland, 9, 32
Political system, 33
Poppo the Monk, 28
Population, 9, 11, 61, 75
    age, 9
    density, 61–62
    growth rate, 9
Power, rise of Swedish, 31–33
Press, free, 33
Prime minister, 34, 41
Princip, Gavrilo, 35
Protestantism, 66
Prussia, 33
Pulp industry. *See* Lumber

R

Railroads, 55, 78
Rape seed, 16
Recipes, 68–69
Refugees, 70, 72, 85
Regions, 13
Reindeer, 22
Religion, 9, 65–67
Rivers, 17, 23
Roman Catholicism, 9, 29, 31
Romani language, 9
Rönnskär, 11
Rosen, Ingrid von, 66
Roskilde Cathedral, 29
Royal

INDEX

Palace, 75
Uppsala Castle, 81
Rurik, 27
Russia, 32, 35

S
Saint Petersburg, 32
Sakgerrak, 7
Salmon, 23
Sami
  language, 9
  people, 9, 22, 62, 63, 64
Samiland, 14
Sawmills, 47–48
Scandinavian Peninsula, 8, 11, 78
Schleswig-Holstein, 38
Seals, 23
Serbia, 35, 64
Shipbuilding, 53
Ships, 25, 55
Siljan lake, 18
Silvia, Queen, 39
Skagerrak strait, 13
Skåne, 15, 16, 52, 53, 61
Skellefte River, 50
Skoghall, 48
Småland, 15
Smörgåsbord, 68, 70
Social
  democratic system, 41
  welfare system, 41, 84, 85
Social Democratic Party, 33, 41, 85
Socialism, 85
Södermanland County, 25
South
  Africa, 71
  Korea, 53
St.
  John the Baptist, 61
  Lucia Day, 69
Standard of living, 41
Steel, 35
Stockholm, 8, 10, 11, 18, 20, 31, 49, 52, 55, 57, 62, 64, 70, 74, 75–76
  Bloodbath, 31
  City Hall (Stadthuset). *See* Gamla Stan (Old Town)
  Palace, 39
Stortoget, 74, 79
Styrbjörn, 28
Suiones, 25, 26
Sundsvall, 19, 47
Svealand (Land of the Swedes), 13, 15
Svenska Handelsbanken, 57
Svensk Bilprovning (Swedish Motor Vehicle Inspection Company), 58
Sverige, 11
Swedish
  language, 9
  meatballs, 68
Sweons, 26
Syria, 9, 59

T
Tacitus, 25
Taxes, 33, 85
Terrain, 7
Timber. *See* Lumber
Torneälven, 17
Tourism, 83
Transportation, 55
Treaties of Rome, 43
Treaty of Paris, 43
Trelleborg, 55
Trysilelva river, 17

U
Ulvaeus, Björn, 71
Umeaälven river, 17
UNESCO World Heritage Site, 50
Unification with Denmark and Norway, 30
United
  Kingdom, 51, 71
  States, 33, 35, 51, 55, 56, 62, 71
University, 65
UN Refugee Agency (UNHCR), 72
Uppsala, 80–81
  University, 80–81
Urbanization, 62, 75

Vaermland, 36
Vänern lake, 48, 49
Värrmland County, 46
Västernorrland, 41
Västra Götaland County, 18, 20
Västrarnorrland County, 19
Vättern lake, 18, 44
Venice, 75
Viking Age, 26–28
Vikings, 25, 26–27
Visby, 55
Volvo, 89
Voting, 33

Wars, 32, 33
Wealth, 35, 38, 56, 85
Welfare state, 85–86
West Germany, 42, 43
Wind power, 85
World Economic Forum, 89
World War
  I, 35, 62
  II, 35, 36, 37–38, 42, 43, 47, 62

Yiddish language, 0
Ynglinga saga, 27
Yugoslavia, 64

Zinc, 50

95

Picture Credits

All images in this book are in the public domain or have been supplied under license by © Shutterstock.com. The publisher credits the following images as follows:

Page 8: Michael715, page 11: Olof Bergqvist, page 20: VanderWolf Images, page 39: 360b, page 42: Roman Yanushevsky, pages 44, 49: allanw, page 48: Imfoto, page 57: Ukko, page 58: Amy Laughinghouse, page 61: Sussi Hj, page 63: V Belov, pages 18, 62: Rolf_52, page 64: Katatonia82, page 67: WDnet Creation, page 70: Bellena, page 72, 88: Stefan Holm,
page 79: Matyas Rehak.
Page 71: Wikimedia Commons.

To the best knowledge of the publisher, all images not specifically credited are in the public domain. If any image has been inadvertently uncredited, please notify the publisher, so that credit can be given in future printings.

Video Credits

Page 12 TheSwedishLad!: http://x-qr.net/1EQ6
page 26 Top Tenz: http://x-qr.net/1FSU
page 65 Andrew Bourne http://x-qr.net/1FWu
page 76 BookingHunterTV: http://x-qr.net/1EfD

Author

Dominic J. Ainsley is a freelance writer on history, geography, and the arts and the author of many books on travel. His passion for traveling dates from when he visited Europe at the age of ten with his parents. Today, Dominic travels the world for work and pleasure, documenting his experiences and encounters as he goes. He lives in the south of England in the United Kingdom with his wife and two children.